NESTS

Some birds build
their nests in trees.

Some birds build
their nests on cliffs.

Some birds build
their nests on the ground.

Some birds build
their nests in holes.

Some birds build
their nests in buildings.

Some birds build
their nests on water.

Why do birds build nests?

Birds build nests
to keep their eggs
and babies safe.